Baptized in Sweet Tea

A Collection of Ken Burger's Columns Celebrating the South

With photography by **David Gentry**

EVENING POST BOOKS
Our Accent is Southern!
www.EveningPostBooks.com

Published by
Evening Post Books
Charleston, South Carolina
www.EveningPostBooks.com

Editor: Holly Holladay
Design: Gill Guerry
Photographer: David Gentry

Fourth printing 2014
Printed in the United States of America by Sun Printing Inc.

A CIP catalog record for this book has been applied
for from the Library of Congress.

ISBN: 978-0-9834457-2-2

TO ALL
SOUTHERN
MOTHERS

INDEX

FOREWORD

You don't have to be born and raised in South Carolina to love and appreciate the subtle and spectacular beauty of the Palmetto State, but it helps.

When I was growing up in one of our many small towns, I came to know that our beloved state is really one big small town, a "cousinry" if you will, made up of people who are related through blood, marriage, business, agriculture, and a common history.

Whether it's a cobblestone street in Charleston, an office building in Columbia, or an old Indian trail through the Piedmont, South Carolina is a place of personality and passion.

This book, in a small way, presents a literary snapshot of what it was like to grow up here and what it means to live here.

Even our new neighbors from the north are quick to realize that ours is a kinder, gentler way to live, which is why they move here. And, of course, why the rest of us stay here.

So enjoy this trip through my home state, warts and all, and don't forget to try the sweet tea. Like most things in South Carolina, it grows on you.

SOUTHERN WAYS

Baptized in Sweet Tea

Saturday, May 8, 2010

I am a proud South Carolinian.

I grew up in a small town. Both parents worked. I went to public schools, and I can read and write.

I was 12 before I saw a town larger than Walterboro. My senior trip was a bus ride to Charleston.

We played baseball and football in a field near our house. We caught snakes in an open ditch. I knew boys who didn't wear shoes until we went to high school. My parents sold their car to build the house I was born in.

We attended Swallow Savannah Methodist Church because it was close to our house and we could walk. I put up the hymn numbers before church services. My mother put grape juice in little glasses for Communion. My father sang in the choir. I was baptized in sweet tea.

High school ring

I played junior varsity football and drums in our championship band. My high school ring had a Fighting Tiger on one side and a Confederate flag on the other.

On summer evenings, a truck came through our neighborhood spraying a noxious fog to kill the mosquitoes. As little boys, we rode our bikes through the poisonous soup for the fun of it.

My parents didn't go to college, but my great-grandfather graduated from The Citadel and my grandmother from Coker. My mother was from Bamberg.

I was sentenced to two years at Anderson Junior College because I didn't have a comma in my SAT score. Then I studied abroad, graduating dead last in my class from the University of Georgia, and got a job with a newspaper in Columbia. I came to Charleston after my first divorce.

No Lake City

I've lived in the Upstate, Midlands and Lowcountry. I've been to races in Darlington, Camden and Elloree.

I used to shag at the Pad. I learned to water ski on one ski. I remember the textile leagues. I knew Columbia before the zoo. I've been to Carolina-Clemson games and remember the Bronze Derby. Almost all my wives have been South Carolinians.

I wear Weejuns and eat boiled peanuts. I've been on the Salkehatchie, Savannah, Santee, Wateree, Congaree, Pee Dee, Ashepoo and Combahee rivers and a lot of creeks in between.

I know about the Coburg Cow, The Clock, Big John's, First Week, the Rocket at the State Fair, The Beacon, and the Big Peach outside Gaffney. I knew Pawleys Island before it was arrogant and Edisto in the good old days.

I've been to the Newberry Opera House, rode the roller coaster in Myrtle Beach, hitchhiked through Orangeburg after the shootings, loaded watermelons in Yemassee and know there is no lake in Lake City.

For all this, I am grateful and consider myself blessed to live in the Palmetto State.

Southern Boys Are Huggers

Sunday, October 24, 2010

If you are new to the area, having moved here from "off," there's something you need to know about Southern boys.

We're huggers.

We hug our old friends, new friends, teammates, enemies, hunting dogs, aunts, uncles, cousins, ex-wives, people we just met, people we don't know and people who just happen to be passing by.

It's because being raised male in the South is to undergo strict and unquestioned basic training on how to be a gentleman.

This simple act of leaning in and feigning a kiss on the cheek is our way of saying we enjoyed meeting you and hope to see you again soon.

It's like a handshake, only better.

But it's understandable that it can catch some people by surprise. Especially in these modern times. We know this is probably not customary where you came from.

But around here, it's the way we do things.

So, please relax. We mean no harm. It's just the way we were raised. We can't help it.

Opening doors

And hugging is just one of the things newcomers have to get used to.

As Southern gentlemen, we're also obsessive about opening doors for ladies. We open office doors, car doors, oven doors, garage doors, trap doors, refrigerator doors, whatever kind of doors need opening.

Of course we know you are perfectly capable of opening a door by yourself, but there's something in our wiring that says if we allow a lady to open a door we will be struck by lightning, or worse, scolded by our mothers.

Oh, and we also give up our seats whenever a lady is left standing in this world of musical chairs.

I even do that when I'm riding a bus or subway in big cities like New York or Washington, which makes people look at me with extreme suspicion, like I'm up to something.

Actually, I'm just doing what I was taught to do.

And this behavior is so deeply ingrained in my DNA that I would jump off the bus or train before I would let a lady stand when I'm seated.

Unquestioned custom

Another thing we do is walk on the traffic side of the sidewalk whenever strolling with a lady.

I always thought this was an interesting gesture, considering it puts us closer to the traffic so we get hit by a passing car rather than exposing the woman to such danger.

As always, I never questioned the custom because it was simply part of our training in how to be a Southern gentleman.

The problem is these little niceties can be off-putting to people who are not accustomed to such unabashed chivalry.

On occasion, we are chastised and lectured about equality and made to feel like we did something wrong.

Personally, I think these people just need a hug.

Seersucker Suits Make a Statement

Saturday, September 12, 2009

Nobody doesn't notice when you're wearing a seersucker suit.

With their lightweight look and somewhat rumpled appearance, these pinstriped summer suits are a trademark of the Southern gentleman, a statement to the world that you're a little different and darned proud of it.

But as common as they are in the Lowcountry of South Carolina, I get those strange looks from people when I wear mine up North, where they're about as common as good manners.

From the moment you walk into a room, people nod in your direction. The suit itself is enough to turn heads.

When you say you're from Charleston, they get this magnolia and lemonade look in their eyes as if you just said you were from Mars.

"All males born in South Carolina," I explain, "are issued a seersucker suit at birth."

I think they believe me.

Mark Twain

I like to wear my gray, pinstriped seersucker suit with an open-collared shirt and a pair of cordovan Bass Weejuns with no socks.

But that's me. Some prefer the light blue pinstripe. There are even pink and tan models for the adventurous.

Andy Griffith wore seersucker suits with suspenders on his long-running TV show "Matlock." Even Barney Fife looked good in a seersucker suit with a straw hat and a bow tie when he was off-duty in Mayberry.

Lots of U.S. senators wore seersucker suits in Washington, D.C., back before air conditioning.

Seersucker is also the suit of choice among Broad

17

Street lawyers during the long summers here in the Holy City.

The most famous attorney to wear a three-piece seersucker suit, of course, was Atticus Finch in the movie "To Kill A Mockingbird."

Quite honestly, there's just something about wearing seersucker that makes you feel like you're starring in a James Dickey novel and talking to Mark Twain while having a drink with William Faulkner.

That's not to say women don't enjoy the light and airy feel of a good seersucker suit. Indeed, the Navy once issued seersucker uniforms to its nurses who served in the warmer climates around the globe.

Wearing newspaper

That's because the all-cotton suits are made in such a way that they facilitate air circulation, a necessity for the well-dressed man or woman on some of our steamiest days of summer.

Back when Britain had its far-flung colonial kingdom, seersucker was a quite popular look in places like India and Burma.

Its sometimes puckered appearance causes some to think it's cheap. My favorite line came from sports

writer Damon Runyon, who said his seersucker suit was causing much confusion among his New York friends. "They cannot decide whether I'm broke or just setting a new vogue."

For me, wearing my seersucker suit is like wearing a newspaper. It's light and easy to read.

Even from a distance it says something about the wearer, something you can't say in a blue blazer or a black tuxedo.

To be sure, there is a time and place for everything when it comes to fashion. And there are those who contend that white bucks and seersucker suits should not be worn after Labor Day.

But here in the Palmetto State, we stretch the calendar out a little longer, allowing them until the first leaf falls in October.

The Poetry of College Football

Sunday, August 24, 2008

I know you're out there, clutching your season tickets, counting the days, deciding what to wear, wondering if it'll be hot or cold, if it will rain, waiting, somewhat impatiently, for the college football season to finally begin.

From big towns and small, all at once, you'll emerge from the back roads, onto the interstates, like migrating herds, dogged, determined, flying the colors, caravans of cars and vans, stocked to the gills with potato salad and fried chicken, sweet tea by the gallon, soft drinks, hard drinks and just enough deviled eggs to go around twice.

It's an ageless procession of frat boys and pretty girls, sorority sisters, old and young, near and dear, distinguished alums, loud mouth louts, children in cheerleader uniforms, drunks in T-shirts and ties, tossing footballs and talking trash.

Then with folding chairs, tightly circled, in dusty lots and grassy fields, perfectly parked, acre upon endless acre, color coordinated, anxious and antsy, fiddling with satellite dishes and scraping paper plates while waiting for shadows to fall and stadium lights to illuminate the dark sky, officially turning game day into night.

Smoke and fire

Once inside, stacked to the stars, elbow to elbow, buying programs and popcorn, stepping over each other, excuse me, excuse me, please and thank you, what a night, what a sight, sure hope the home team wins.

And they might, or not, depending on the truth, and rumors, about sophomore tackles and redshirt quarterbacks and what the coach had to say about so-and-so last week.

A few boos for the visiting varmints, jumping jacks and leg lifts, practice punts that hang high in the lights, falling softly onto the cool wet grass, chewed up by the cleats of cutting cornerbacks, double checking coverage, assignments, and girlfriends gabbing in the grandstands.

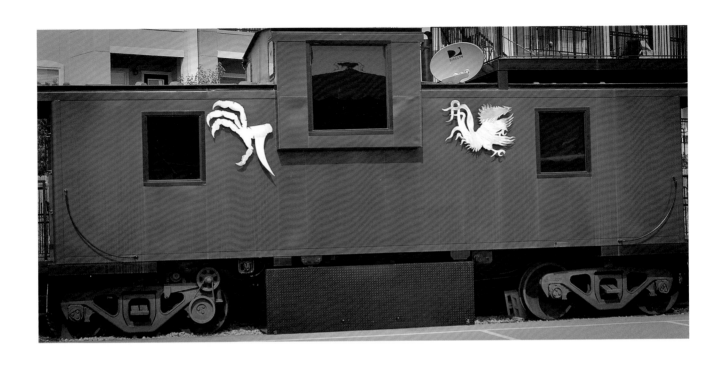

Then down the hill and through the tunnel they come, smoke and cannon fire, combined to thrill and quicken pulses, gladiators in the arena, trotting, taunting, to the beat of a drum major, high-stepping, bringing the band and its audience to a chilling crescendo.

Pain and passion

Awash in the ebb and flow, a touchdown here, a field goal there, the game unfolds, the good, the bad, for better or worse, damn the luck, and the referees, not to mention the tailback who fumbled on the one.

Screaming helps, but you've got to pee, too much sweet tea, maybe later, in the second half, when the lines aren't long, when only true believers are left, holding hands, singing alma maters in the rain.

Win or lose the traffic's tough, sitting still, inching nowhere, as the coach comes on the radio, explaining himself, finding victory in defeat, looking ahead to next week, next year, when things will be better, or worse, he really doesn't know.

But it's all brought to you by somebody's hot dog chili, perfect for tailgating, and the local bank that loves the home team, and you, the faithful fan, whose family's needs are always met by a former field goal kicker turned insurance salesman.

In the aftermath comes analysis, talk of change, pain, promise and passion, for the game, the team, the common cause.

Back home the flags are stowed and pretty pennants put away, for another day, of hope and heartbreak, in those precious hours of fun, fashion and fancy called college football.

Loving Where We Live

Tuesday, May 25, 2010

As the afternoon sun sinks slowly behind the western edge of the creek, a johnboat slips silently upstream, a few feet from a great blue heron, just beneath the ever-present osprey.

To the right, a box turtle suns himself on the sagging limb of a tree that leaned too close to the water's edge. To the left, a red-winged black bird chirps a warning then flies away.

Up ahead, the brackish water winds like a serpent, slowly seeking a slope that barely exists.

Pushed by the imperceptible hands of time, it follows ancient commands like a soldier, without question, without knowing why, or where it all ends.

There is something special about being in the waterways of the Lowcountry, surrounded by silence, except for the rustling of birds and the subtle sway of spartina grass.

They say people come here for the beaches. But they stay here for the marsh.

Hidden gardens

When you think of the South Carolina Lowcountry, the mind is flooded with visions of sun-drenched days on long sandy beaches, carriage rides down romantic lanes or moss-covered trees swaying softly in an afternoon breeze.

Throughout this mosaic you hear the sounds of summer. Shag music coming off a sandbar. Children's voices escaping the boundaries of a schoolyard. People talking as they turn a corner and fade off into hidden gardens. Church bells chiming across the city, signaling the passage of time, a commodity measured differently here somehow.

Then there are the restaurants, bars, museums, parks, vistas and sunsets that seem painted by hands unknown and unseen.

From the billowing sails on the harbor to the eternal patience of a cane-pole fisherman dangling a hook from a shady bridge along a country road, there is a peace that prevails and should never be taken for granted.

Freshly spanked

Some days this feels like an old place, moss-covered, storied, sinking slowly into a Confederate grave where it will lie comfortably with those whose lives and names have come and gone.

But some days it feels newborn, pink, freshly spanked, and ready to take on new ways of doing old things.

Because we're not without traffic, crime, and people who don't know how to behave. Thus we have not excused ourselves from society at large.

We simply long to be small enough to see the daily wonders, enjoy the sweetness of shade, smell the magnolia blooms, glide home on an incoming tide, pull up to the dock just as the last rays of day descend behind the tall pines, and be thankful that we love where we live.

An Act of Final Respect

Thursday, April 14, 2011

I saw the procession coming down King Street and pulled over to the side of the road.

Behind the long black hearse was a line of cars, headlights on, some filled with immediate family, the rest with friends, co-workers, church members and neighbors, as the final parade of a life passed slowly by.

Without thinking, I automatically slowed and stopped, a practice I witnessed more than a hundred times when I was growing up.

White, black, didn't matter.

Granted, it's harder to do in a city where a person's last ride is often lost in rush-hour traffic. But if you grew up in rural America, you were taught this was an act of final respect, whether you knew the deceased or not.

I'm sure I didn't fully appreciate this gesture when I was young, but it means much more to me now.

Old habits

Indeed, old habits are hard to break.

It's like waving to people you don't know, speaking to strangers, or placing your hand on the shoulder of someone in need of a human touch.

These were some of the little things we were taught to do, out of human kindness and dignity, regardless of race, creed, or color.

Here in the South, we're often painted with the broad brush of racism. Sometimes it's deserved. Mostly, however, it isn't.

I grew up in the segregated South, and it certainly wasn't pretty, even from the white side of the fence. You didn't have to be a scholar to know reality did not reflect the words of independence and equality we studied in school.

In life, I learned, there will always be a disparate dispensation among people.

But in death, equality evens the score.

Mutual respect

This week's recollections of what brought about America's Civil War is a time for everyone with a Southern accent and heritage to reflect on the past, consider the consequences, and look ahead to the future.

All of us, regardless of skin color, have a stake in what we teach our children and grandchildren about what has come before. Because hatred, like love, is taught at the knee of elders and passed along for the next generation to employ.

While we are not personally responsible for discrimination in the past, neither are we immune to the pain of the present, or blind to the distrust that shadows our future.

Beyond the ceremonial cannon fire, behind the uniformed actors, beneath the scolding of some, and because we breathe the same air, we will all someday ride in that long line of cars en route to the same end.

Whether or not we slow down, pull over and show each other the mutual respect earned from living and dying on this earth, is what ultimately decides our equality as human beings.

SMALL TOWN FOLK

Our State Is One Big Small Town

Thursday, December 9, 2010

If you grew up in the Palmetto State, you know that South Carolina is a collection of small towns connected by country roads, family ties, and stories, true or false, passed along between friends and foes.

When you're young, of course, your corner of the world is the entire world as far as you're concerned.

Mine was the swampy shallows along the Savannah River, in the southwestern part of the state, an area dotted with towns that pretty much peaked in the 1960s.

I often say we competed in the Hyphenated Conference, because all the high schools had names like Allendale-Fairfax, Denmark-Olar, Williston-Elko, Bamberg-Ehrhardt and Blackville-Hilda.

The towns were so small they had to be lumped together in order to make a school big enough to exist.

Some, like Langley-Bath-Clearwater and Hunter-Kinard-Tyler, actually required two hyphens.

Drinking buddies

Once you grew up, went off to school, got a job and a grip on how diverse our lovely state really is, you came to understand that it's all interconnected by old family loyalties, fraternity friends, sorority sisters, ex-wives, former brothers-in-law, business relations, beach houses, river trips, political enemies, Civil War stories and things that make us all distant cousins in this dysfunctional family tree with roots that run from the mountains to the sea.

If you're from Charleston, for instance, you probably have relatives in Newberry, perhaps a college roommate from Myrtle Beach, a former girlfriend from Florence, an old drinking buddy from Anderson, a cousin or two from Beaufort and a friend with a hunting lodge outside Saluda.

People who went to Clemson have a friendly dislike for people who went to South Carolina, but they all know folks who used to grow tobacco in Pamplico, some who worked at the Bomb Plant outside Aiken, others who grew up in Gaffney, and a few who never left Aynor.

Hypnotizing chickens

Through marriages, divorces, dove shoots, land disputes, house parties, Boys State, military schools, lawsuits, family reunions, summer jobs, business mergers and midnight drag races, we're all just one question away from knowing somebody who knows somebody who knows somebody you know.

You've probably had conversations that begin with, "If you're from Blacksburg, you probably know that sorry son-of-a-gun so-and-so."

That's usually followed by a remark like, "Well, I didn't know him, but his brother from Spartanburg was good friends with my uncle from Cross Anchor who married one of those twins from Andrews who turned out to be first cousins with my sister's maid of honor in her first wedding to a guy named Bubba from Bamberg who ended up going to jail for shooting a shrimper from Frogmore because he didn't pay up on a bet that he could hypnotize a chicken."

Truth is, if you can diagram that sentence, for better or worse, you're a genuine South Carolinian.

Raised By a Hundred Mothers

Sunday, May 10, 2009

In small towns, you're never out of your mother's sight. Or somebody else's mother's.

In today's world, you're lucky to have one mother, much less a hundred. But that's the way it was when I was a kid.

No matter where you were or what you were doing, you were always under the watchful eye of a collective group of women who took it upon themselves to raise each other's children.

While there was no formal contract to do so, it was understood that they all had equal powers of discipline when it came to your behavior.

Whether you were standing in the lunch line at school or sitting in a pew at church, one wrong move and somebody's mother was there to straighten you out.

Even when my mom was working, it was not unusual for a close friend's mother to call out my full name, Kenneth Nolan Burger, across the playground if I was out of line.

That's when you knew you were in real trouble.

Permission to punish

Sometime soon after giving birth, mothers automatically acquire this mid-octave range in their voice that can stop a child cold in his tracks.

It's somewhere between shrill and accusatory: you know it when you hear it and you freeze.

Because in those small, tight-knit communities, there was no place to hide.

All the mothers had that voice of authority and they knew how to use it.

Not only that, they had permission to punish. I dare

say I got as many spankings outside the home as I did inside the home. And deserved every one of them.

Fathers, of course, were important. They served as role models, taught us how to hit a baseball and slide into second.

But when the games were over and hearts needed mending, it was the mothers who dried the tears, bandaged the wounds and made sure there was homemade ice cream for the winning and losing teams.

Super women

I can still see them, actually, standing around the churchyard, talking away, lipstick and ear bobs in place, one hand directing traffic and the other grabbing a child by the collar, whispering some unknown threat in his ear.

I think I feared other people's mothers more than my own. They had a way of making you feel like you disappointed the entire town.

It was that universal expectation that made us all accountable.

But these women could also lift you up, dust you off, wipe your nose, dry your eyes and send you out to play when things seemed hopeless.

Even when I wandered into territory considered to be the wrong side of the tracks, there were kindhearted women who ignored color barriers, watched out for me and made sure I made it home safely.

Looking back, they were truly super women. They worked full time, sang in the choir, volunteered at the school, taught us to dance, held our families together and somehow found time to raise a village full of children.

To have one such mother is a special thing, indeed. To have a hundred is the gift of a lifetime.

Dr. Luke, A Family Physician

Saturday, February 21, 2009

I have been blessed with many distinctions, but only one has been with me all my life.

I was the first baby that Dr. Luke Laffitte delivered so many years ago in Allendale, the small town where I grew up. The first of more than 3,000 babies he brought into the world.

He had just graduated from the Medical College of South Carolina and returned to his home county. This was in another era, a thousand years ago, when small towns still grew their own doctors. Everybody called him Dr. Luke.

As fate would have it, they were still building the county hospital when my mother informed the young physician she was about to give birth. He said he would meet her at the Orangeburg Hospital, 45 miles away, when the time came.

She said no way.

Thus I was born at home, in the corner bedroom, in the house I grew up in until I left for college. It was my mother's second such experience, but it was Dr. Luke's first.

And neither of us has ever forgotten it.

The first

It's nice to be known as the first for something in your life. It doesn't happen very often.

So every time I would see Dr. Luke we would laugh about it. I always joked that he got better at delivering babies as time went on.

During my childhood Dr. Luke stitched up my many wounds and treated me when I was sick. He was a bundle of energy, treating blacks and whites with equal tenderness, even when they had to enter through separate entrances in the old days.

41

He even made house calls, something people today have only heard about. I remember him coming to our house late at night, with his little black bag and a smile that never showed how tired he was.

Like most country doctors, he was often paid in kind. Sometimes it was a load of fresh vegetables on his back porch. Sometimes it was meat in his freezer. Sometimes not at all.

He said my birth cost $35 and my parents paid him $5 a week until the bill was settled.

A healer

I saw Dr. Luke this week and held his hand, reminding him how far we both had traveled down this road of life.

He didn't say much, but he knew I was there. He's 85 years old and looks small in the hospital bed down at Medical University Hospital.

I only hope the nurses and doctors whizzing past his room know how special he is, how many lives he's touched and saved and brought into the world.

I hope they're not too busy to realize that the gray-haired gentleman behind all the tubes and machines is one of them, a healer, a small-town doctor who never knew a stranger.

Way too many of our rural communities exist without adequate health care these days, much less a loving doctor who lives among them. It's a sad sign of the times.

Country doctors like Dr. Luke didn't get as rich as big-city doctors, but I bet he had more friends.

Personally, I appreciate him bringing me into this world and hope he sticks around a little longer. We've come a long way together, Dr. Luke. Godspeed.

Remembering Ed and Marlene

Thursday, February 25, 2010

Bright neon signs glowed eerily through nights as dark as the loamy soil in the river-bottom world we lived in.

A string of mom-and-pop motels and locally owned restaurants stretched like Christmas tree lights, bait laid out on a lonely stretch of U.S. Highway 301 to catch tourists migrating from New York to Florida, and back again, as predictable as summer thunderstorms.

One such place was the Carolina Diner, a cinder-block building on the north side of Allendale, not much bigger than the sign itself, a hangout where locals passed those restless times known as the teen years.

By day it served as a meat-and-three lunch stop for county agents, insurance salesmen and passersby who wanted a taste of collard greens and candied yams.

But at night it transformed, magically, into a paradise where young boys smoked in public and Pabst Blue Ribbon beer flowed like water in a wishing well where we tossed our dreams and waited impatiently for them to come true.

Surrogate parents

My parents were wonderful people, hard workers, churchgoers, but they were not cool.

In every small town there was one couple who walked that social tight rope between responsibility and rebellion and made it look easy.

In our town, it was Ed and Marlene Mixson.

They owned and operated the diner, switching from meatloaf and mashed potatoes at lunch to hamburgers and happy hour at night.

Marlene was a beauty who smoked Chesterfields and possessed an I-mean-it look that could back down barking dogs and turn hotheads into apologetic angels in an instant.

Ed was an eternal entrepreneur who dabbled in politics and brought an air of sophistication to the farming community with a cigarette holder that placed him on par with FDR in our book.

Together they served as surrogate parents to a flock of kids serving time behind the Palmetto State's pine curtain, preparing us for flight into whatever lay beyond the darkness.

Innocence lost

Mostly, though, I remember the laughter.

It was the unlisted staple on a limited menu they seldom bothered to bring to the table.

Because we already knew what we wanted.

We wanted freedom and that fraternal feeling you get when you know everybody and everybody knows you.

On summer nights we would sit outside on the hoods of cars, underage, under-stimulated and under-whelmed by the life we yearned to leave.

Ed and Marlene were strict enough to keep the riff-raff away and lenient enough to sell a boy his first beer a few days before his 18th birthday, as long as nobody told his parents the next morning in church.

I miss the innocence of the hours we spent at the diner, pining for brighter lights and bigger adventures.

And I miss Ed and Marlene, the parents who helped guide us from adolescence to adulthood under the neon lights on those very dark nights so long, long ago.

Things My Mother Used To Say

Sunday, March 22, 2009

My mother, rest her soul, was a Southern lady who had a way with words.

I often listen to South Carolina's women and the way they talk, falling under their spell like an old man in a hammock.

Not only is their rhythm as lazy as a summer day, but a sense of something long gone.

No matter what they're saying, it always sounds somewhat sinister, a little bit bawdy, kind of concerned and very important.

Growing up in a small town, I had a hundred mothers, and they all talked with a sameness I thought would last forever. And it wasn't just the way they said the words, but the words themselves.

"I do declare," was one of my mother's favorite off-hand expressions. It served her well, whether it was news of an aunt coming down with the flu or the end of World War II.

"Gracious goodness," was another exclamatory remark that seemed to fit, be it the demise of the family dog or the fact that it might rain.

The difference between life and death, it seems, was simply in the inflection.

I swannee

One of my favorite expressions came when my mother didn't quite know what to make of something. She'd just nod her head knowingly and say, "Well, I swannee."

Now, we weren't anywhere near the Suwannee River in Florida or the university in Sewanee, Tenn.

So my guess is this was just a modified Methodist version of "I swear."

Southern ladies, of course, didn't swear. So when she

49

was somewhere between approval and disapproval, she would shake her head and say, "I swannee for goodness."

My mother was smart, valedictorian of her class at Bamberg High School, plus a year of secretarial school. She could read and write with the best of them. But she could also talk with the least of them.

There were times when I couldn't tell if she was talking to me or the maid when she'd let go with, "Well, I sho 'nuf reckon that could be true, Annie Lou."

You gotta love a woman who can talk like that.

Old Weejuns

"Do Lord" was another common response. Everybody within spitting distance of the church used this term to let the world know there was a power greater than themselves at work in the world.

Thinking back on these country expressions reminds me of what it was like to be a little boy listening to adults talk. The conversations weren't that far removed from Gullah.

When I'm hanging around old friends from my hometown, I quickly slide into sayings I haven't used in years. When that happens, it's like putting on an old pair of Weejuns.

These are comfort expressions that we grew up with. We wouldn't use them in business conversations today. But they are part of us, like the hymns we sang in church or the nursery rhymes we learned in school.

No doubt, I'm still that little boy who followed his mother around town, listening to her gossip and carry on small talk in our small-town world.

And all I can say about it now is, "merciful heavens," I miss her.

This One's for You, Harry

Sunday, November 8, 2009

WASHINGTON — The seat next to me was empty.

As the first Lowcountry Honor Flight carried about a hundred World War II vets to the nation's capital to visit their long-overdue memorial, one of them couldn't make it at the last minute.

Just as well, because I was making this trip for Harry, my father, who didn't live to see this day. The empty seat made it feel like he was along for the ride.

And he would have been proud, almost seven decades after the fact, that his generation was getting this kind of special attention. But like those who did make this journey, his humility would not have let him show it.

"It's kind of strange getting honored for something you did so long ago," Gordon Grant of Hilton Head Island said as firetrucks formed a welcoming arch of water upon their arrival here at Ronald Reagan Washington National Airport.

But the planeload of veterans, mostly in their 80s, got used to the attention. As they deplaned, they were met with a brass band and a long line of people applauding their arrival.

Even Harry would have smiled.

Over there

Harry Burger was like most of these vets; he joined the fight shortly after Pearl Harbor.

Dad told us he volunteered for tank duty because he didn't want to walk. But there must have been moments when he wondered about that decision.

During the war, he rose in rank to be a commander in Gen. George S. Patton's Sixth Armored Division. But that's about all we know.

Like most children of combat veterans, my brother and I never heard much about what happened over there.

53

Guys like Harry came home, went to work and never talked about the war.

We inherited an old army footlocker with some letters he wrote to our mother from France. There was a Nazi flag, a silver star and a bronze star, but that's about it.

We know he received a battlefield commission, but he said he got it because everybody else got killed.

I always wondered what he did with all those horrible memories. They weren't in the footlocker.

Real heroes

Such is the legacy for most of the Greatest Generation. Only recently, in their waning days, have we decided we missed the boat when it came to honoring what they accomplished.

On this sun-splashed Saturday in our nation's capital, 10 other flights came loaded with World War II survivors from other states. While there were some walkers, canes and hearing aids, these veterans were remarkable in their sturdiness and stamina.

It was a long day, filled with tours of monuments to every war we've ever fought. But each step of the way, the folks who run Honor Flight made sure they were regaled with thank-yous for their service to our country.

A humble bunch, these men and a few women were clearly touched when they arrived at the memorial that recognized their efforts, the 400,000 who died for the cause and the millions who passed on before this kind of recognition began.

Mostly, these old warriors just feel lucky they made it back alive. And they've done a lot of living since. They've raised families, built a nation and retired to live out their golden years in peace.

Almost all will tell you the war was the greatest adventure of their lives, but the real heroes never came home.

Broke down

Just to be around these veterans is to relive history. Indeed, there's a story behind every handshake.

Throughout the day, there were conversations about submarines, aircraft carriers, landing craft and paratroopers. And in quiet moments, among themselves, they talked about Okinawa, Iwo Jima, Normandy and a hundred other battles you never heard of. And yet, to them, the memories are still vivid.

This program, Lowcountry Honor Flight (www.honorflightlowcountry.com), brings honor to those who never sought plaudits for doing what had to be done. And it couldn't happen without contributions and many volunteers who serve as guardians for the vets.

It also has a time element. The next flight is in April. And they will do the flights until there are no more veterans to honor.

But the day was theirs and theirs alone. Everywhere they went, people stopped and thanked them. Bands played. There were police escorts. And every now and then, there was a tear.

And just when they thought it was all over, they arrived back in Charleston to hundreds of people cheering, bagpipes playing and military honor guards snapping to attention.

Don Pounder, a Navy veteran from Mount Pleasant, said the whole experience was simply overwhelming.

"When I heard the national anthem today I simply broke down and cried," he said. "I've never seen anything like this in my life."

Which, of course, is the purpose behind the Honor Flights. I just wish Harry could have come along for the ride.

Going Home for Funerals

Sunday, January 9, 2011

ALLENDALE — The church was much smaller than I remembered, but then again, everything seems that way when you go home for funerals.

Separated by 90 miles and more than 40 years, visits to this little town in the pine forests of South Carolina always bring back memories of a youth freckled with optimism and splashed with the sunshine of tomorrow.

Now, it's an all-too-often trek back to pay respects to those who made it that way.

Last week the little Episcopal church was packed for Margaret Boylston, a beloved teacher and role model for a generation of post-war babies.

At 91, she had lived the small-town life to its fullest, raising two boys and a high school full of would-be world-changers.

Some did, some didn't, but everyone came back to say how much they cared for the lady who helped us along the way.

Full circle

As we gathered, gray-haired and balding, we realized life was coming full circle, that this was not the last time we would meet under the moss-draped oaks of Swallow Savannah Cemetery to leave behind another memory.

We laughed that we had to stop meeting like this, but solemnly agreed it would only get worse in the years to come.

The world we knew had changed, for better or worse. And the people who lived down the street and around the corner, the ones who towered above our lives, gave us strength and hope, were slowly but surely slipping away.

In her last years, I remember my own mother saying, "You don't realize you're old until you look around and there's no one who remembers you as a child."

That reality becomes more chilling with each service I attend.

Pretending

Afterwards, between bites of triangle sandwiches and chicken wings, we milled around Mrs. Boylston's house as if she might be sitting in the next room, waiting to talk to us.

As a drama teacher, she taught us how to pretend. And so we did, as we always do when we come home, wishing it was still the way it was.

But, of course, it's not.

Strangers live in the house where I was born. The ball fields are overgrown. The high school is a middle school, and the football stadium that loomed so large on Friday nights looks small and insignificant.

Meanwhile, a logging truck rumbles by, dropping its crumbling cargo on the highway. Stores that once flourished are closed, and Main Street is quiet, except for a freight train that drags slowly through town.

Traces of our youth still exist, but they are rusted and sag under the weight of time and distance.

Only the smiles that spread across familiar faces make you feel like you're home again, at least for a little while, until we gather again.

BOYS WILL BE BOYS

Hot Cars and Hot Summers

Sunday, May 30, 2010

I come from an age when cars had bucket seats, stick shifts, double-barreled carburetors and no air conditioning.

These were the days when cooling the inside of an automobile robbed horsepower from those mighty mills that hurled us like rockets through the muggy nights of South Carolina summers.

I grew up when cars were more than transportation. They were symbols of a society possessed with power, when speed limits were subtle suggestions, when seat belts were for sissies and nobody ever got arrested for driving under the influence of obsession.

Those were the days when cars had names like GTO, 442, Sport Fury, Mustang, 409, Road Runner, SS 396, Cobra, Camaro, Challenger, Barracuda, Firebird, Trans Am, Superbird, GTX, Charger and Hemi.

It was an era of cheap gas, hood scoops, lake pipes, speed shifting, drag racing, mag wheels and growling, guttural sounds that would wake you up in the middle of the night and make you want to leave home.

Devil-may-care

Today, people consider doing 80 on the interstate pushing the limits, and they are right. Speed kills. We have the statistics and cemeteries to prove it.

How we survived the 1960s while roaring down those dark, rural, narrow, farm-to-market roads is a miracle that can only be explained by God's soft spot for fools.

But speed was a fact of life and death in those days. It was glorified in the manufacture of muscle cars and elevated to a sport on race tracks around the South, where our heroes spun their way through catastrophic crashes and walked away, lit up a cigarette and kissed the beauty queen.

Such were role models in those devil-may-care days.

A deer's breath

I remember one summer night, high on humidity, when we were driving faster than our headlights could pierce the darkness, when telephone poles flew by like fence posts, the driver had one hand on the gear shift, was using the other to light up a smoke, the speedometer was pegged, and we were still accelerating.

With all the insight of a 16-year-old, I thought I was finally living, when in reality I was a deer's breath from dying.

Having survived such a reckless youth, I now drive with both hands on the wheel, reasonably close to the speed limit, seat belt securely fastened, eyes on my mirrors, scanning all directions for somebody who looks like me when I didn't know better.

But I must admit, when a hot car rumbles by, I still want to roll down the windows, let my hair catch the rushing wind and leave the air-conditioned, airbag world of modern cars in the dust.

Bringing in Sounds from Afar

Saturday, January 15, 2011

On starlit evenings, when the wind died down and the atmosphere crackled with static, I slowly turned the dial on my radio in search of those voices in the night.

While other boys tuned into baseball games in faraway places, my ear was aching to hear the melodic tones of Dick Bionde and Cousin Brucie and a handful of other disc jockeys whose voices boomed out from tall towers in places like Chicago, Fort Wayne, New York, Jacksonville and Nashville.

I, of course, had no idea exactly where these places were, or how to get there. All I knew was that they existed on the tiny AM radio I got for Christmas, a beige, plastic apparatus that I would take to my bedroom and use as a spaceship to the stars.

Because if I turned it just right, holding it near my bedroom window, twisting the delicate dial just so, rock and roll music and witty banter came flooding across the lakes and rivers and mountains and pine trees right into my little life, just like I was actually there.

Blowtorches

In these days of satellite radio and music downloaded from the Internet, it's hard to imagine a world so small.

In those days, there were radio stations that had national reach, 50,000-watt blowtorches that sent a clear-channel signal traveling across the country like a sonic boom.

There was WLS in Chicago, WOWO in Fort Wayne, WABC in New York, WAPE in Jacksonville and WLAC in Nashville.

As I slowly twisted the dial, one of these powerhouse stations would suddenly blast into my bedroom, clear as a dinner bell.

This was the 1950s in a world of peace and prosperity, where Andy Williams and Pat Boone were giving way to

Elvis Presley and Jerry Lee Lewis, where Nat King Cole and Bobby Darin existed alongside Bill Haley and The Comets; Danny and The Juniors.

While some boys studied batting averages, I memorized lyrics to "Wake Up Little Susie" by the Everly Brothers and "Chances Are" by Johnny Mathis.

Transistors

This, of course, was just before the world changed, as it always does.

It was a secret place, just beyond the reach of parental control, where I could skip across the dial and find people and places and songs that allowed a glimpse of a life I longed to live; a place where records played and people danced in a non-stop testament to new-found freedom.

All I needed was a transistor radio and a couple of D-cell batteries and I could reach out, snatch music from the sky and hold it close, like a candle in the dark.

On the horizon, of course, were The Beatles, the Rolling Stones and an invasion that would change the world, radio as we knew it and small boys listening to music in the dark.

Confessions of a Student Bus Driver

Tuesday, February 9, 2010

I don't drive with my right hand resting on the gear shift knob for one very good reason — Trooper S.C. Moseley.

In the 1960s, when I went to high school, the Palmetto State used student school bus drivers.

Believe it or not, all you had to do to qualify was be 16 years old, have a valid driver's license and take a week-long course under the tutelage of a South Carolina Highway Patrolman.

The reason behind what sounds like a ridiculous idea was simple economics. Student bus drivers earned a whopping $35 a month, which was enough for a kid back then.

The program also aimed to build character and responsibility among young boys on their way to becoming men.

And, for the most part, it worked.

Lazy shifting

Every day after school we would report to the big yellow bus parked behind the gymnasium and take turns driving it around the parking lot.

Trooper Moseley, a bear of a man, sat in the right-hand front seat barking instructions about stopping at railroad crossings, opening the door, and swinging out the stop sign on the side of the bus.

The worst thing you could do, however, was leave your right hand on the shifter between gears. Trooper Moseley expected you to return both hands to the steering wheel between each gear change.

If you did not follow his specific orders, Trooper Moseley used a wooden yard stick to reach over and rap the back of your right hand sharply as a reminder.

By the time the week was over, the back of my right hand was red from being hit so many times for what the trooper considered lazy shifting.

Norman Rockwell

I look back on those days with amazement. That our state leaders thought a bunch of 16-year-olds could handle the responsibility of driving school buses loaded with our most precious cargo seems quite preposterous in hindsight.

But truthfully, most were responsible citizens who did their duty with dignity, considered it an honor and had something they could put on their resume under "extra-curricular activities" when applying for college.

Granted, it wasn't a perfect system. There were times when we drag-raced big yellow school buses on deserted country roads, even though they would only do 35 mph.

And I stuck one up to the axles in a soybean field one rainy winter day.

But this Norman Rockwell notion of rural America was sure to fade sooner or later.

By 1986 the federal government demanded that the last three states using student bus drivers — South Carolina, North Carolina and Alabama — abandon the practice and transition to adult professionals.

I just hope they had somebody like Trooper Moseley who taught them to keep both hands on the wheel, or else....

You Say Potato, I Say 'Tater'

Tuesday, January 4, 2011

Despite living here in the big city for many years, I'm still a country boy at heart. Which means I can easily slip back into the lazy language I grew up with.

Here in South Carolina, it's somewhere between country bumpkin and Gullah, a combination of words slurred together in order to convey a feeling, an idea or an intention.

For me, it's like falling back into a comfortable chair. There are certain terms that just fit specific occasions or situations.

For those who are still trying to adjust to our cadence and slang, here's a primer that might help you along:

Y'all: A group of people.

All y'all: The plural of y'all.

Gimmedat: Give me that.

Wholenother: Something else altogether.

Nillybout: Nearly about, or almost.

Slapdab: In the middle; or smackdab.

Richeer: Come sit right here.

Hornswoggled: Bamboozled.

Lookaheyuh: Pay attention.

Right Regular: Often.

Fixinta: Getting ready to.

Yonder: A place far away.

Jeet yet?

We also say:

Mash: As in mash the button.

Carry You There: Drive you.

Idnit?: Isn't it?

Compny: Cheap relatives.

Wadjugit?: Vanilla or chocolate?

Caddywampus: Catty-corner, only different.

Sit a spell: Visit.

Liberry: Where books live.

Sairdy: Day after Friday.

Sumptin: Something's up.

Jeet?: Did you eat?

Soft drinks

Other favorites include:

Chimbley: Fireplace.

Srump: Shrimp.

Purtnear: Pretty near.

Sho-nuff: Sure enough.

Chirren: Children.

Dem: Them.

Dat: That.

Hosepipe: Garden hose.

Owie: Ouch.

Reckon: Consider.

Directly: Sooner or later.

If'n: If I could.

Mightcoulda: Might be able to.

Ustacoulda: Was once able to.

Co-Cola: All soft drinks.

Fishing with Nick Gainey

Saturday, May 10, 2008

MONCKS CORNER — Forty-eight bass boats bob about in the waters of the upper Cooper River, waiting for the signal.

Rangers, Skeeters, Stratos and Tritons. Sleek, low-slung boats that bubble with big-old Mercury, Evinrude, Yamaha and Johnson outboards on the back.

Every Thursday afternoon a convoy of good-old boys in muscle trucks appears from every direction, backing their boats down the ramps, down into the brown water where the big-mouth bass play hide and seek beneath the surface.

The parking lot at Cypress Gardens Landing is choreographed chaos, a showcase of boy toys, single-purpose machines made for finding fish in a hurry.

I'm sitting in one of them, a 21-foot Ranger piloted by Nick Gainey, a professional fisherman from Charleston. I know this because his name is on the side of his boat.

At exactly 5:30 p.m., one by one, the boats are sent off in order. When each number is called out over the megaphone, a boat suddenly squats in the water, you hear the noise of the engine and see men waving as they tear out up-river, or down-river, depending on where they think they can find fish.

We are No. 41.

Cheek-flapping fast

When our number is called, Nick pushes his boat out of the pack, up-stream, nose high, water boiling up behind us.

Within seconds the big boat planes out, we see the river stretching out in front of us, the trees along the banks a blur as we lean into the wind.

The 250-horse power Mercury does its job. We go from sitting still to 60 miles per hour in seconds. I quickly stash my hat under the seat before it flies away. I look over at Nick. He's stoic. Sunglasses hide his eyes. A red hat sits tight on his head.

I wonder how he keeps his hat on, but asking questions is out of the question. We're flying. Cheek-flapping fast.

To my amazement, another boat suddenly appears alongside, starboard, and passes us.

Nick stares straight ahead. Everybody has his own destination. Nobody blinks.

Ten minutes later, after carving our way through a maze of unmarked channels, he lets up, the boat relaxes in the water, giving way to the out-going tide.

It's time to fish.

Time is money

Nick Gainey is 63 years old and makes his living in property management. His avocation, however, is fishing, fulltime.

He doesn't drink, smoke, or chew. He fishes.

Eleven months of the year he's on the road, pulling the Ranger to bass tournaments from Alabama to Canada.

He laughs when he tells you the truth. Last year he earned $35,000 fishing and spent $40,000 doing it. He considers that success because he's doing what he loves.

This Thursday afternoon tournament on the Cooper River is strictly local. A working man's tournament. Show up after work, toss 50 bucks in the hat, fish for three hours, see what happens.

The boat with five fish that weigh the most gets a check. Biggest fish also gets paid.

So time is money.

Fishing is serious business.

Old rice fields

We head up the east branch of the Cooper, back where old rice fields stretch for miles and egrets and alligators pay little attention to fast boats flying up and down the river.

Our first stop is near an old stump where a pelican is perched, watching us with amusement. Nick hands me a rod with a brown plastic worm on the end of the line.

He's working a spinner bait close to the bank.

The number of fish I've caught in my lifetime wouldn't feed an osprey for a day. But I understand the concept. Fishing is about fooling the food chain. We are, after all, supposed to be the smart ones.

Nick stands on the bow of the boat, casting, reeling, casting again.

I manage to get my bait wet a few times, but nothing happens.

A steady breeze out of the south ripples the water and makes the fishing hard. At least that's what Nick keeps mumbling.

By the time I get the hang of it, it's time to move to another spot.

Brown plastic worm

At the second spot we float deeper into a rice field, careful not to disturb another boat nearby.

Within minutes Nick hooks a fish that bends his rod, flaps on the water and glistens in the slanting sunlight as he lifts it up and drops it into the box onboard. A two-pounder. Maybe more.

He switches to a top-water plug and catches another, smaller fish. I keep dragging my brown plastic worm

through the water. Determined. Dogged. Undeterred. Fishing is all about patience. Sort of.

We're fishing against the clock. Three hours. Not much time when the sun is setting and the livewell is empty.

Nick is working hard, racing from one spot to another, changing baits, sliding us left and right with the trolling motor, looking for fish.

Once I toss my tackle too close to a big blue heron who squawks and flies away, seemingly annoyed by the presence of a rookie on his beloved river.

Can't say that I blame him.

Fish stories

Landlubbers are always amazed at how much water there is around here.

What we see from the bridges hardly fills a bait bucket compared to the vast river reaches of the Lowcountry.

Whether you catch a fish or not, the scenery is worth the trip into the wild waters that wind for miles and miles into a world we seldom see.

All you need to do is spend an afternoon with the river rats up in Berkeley County to get a renewed appreciation.

With the sun setting, Nick guns the boat back home. Soon we are joined in the main channel by other boats, running lights on, riding in each other's wake, making our way home as darkness draws down on the day.

As we all converge on the landing at the same time, the traffic is heavy. Fish are being weighed. Boats are being hauled out of the water, fast and furious.

It's no place for a man who can't back a boat trailer.

All told, Nick and I combine for two fish at just over three pounds.

He caught two. I caught none.

A couple of guys sluice their slippery catch into the bucket and tip the scales at 17 pounds. We wish them well, load up and head home as fish stories fill the evening air behind us.

The Art of Using Cusswords

Tuesday, January 11, 2011

I never heard my daddy cuss.

He was a war veteran who supervised a warehouse full of blue-collar workers, but not once in my life did I hear him let go with a string of expletives.

Not so his youngest son.

Beyond earshot of my non-cursing parents, I learned a plethora of off-color words that became part of my vocabulary at an early age.

In fact, as little boys, we used to take great pride in using new words we learned to say, even if we didn't know what they meant.

By the time we were in high school, we could rattle off a disgusting diatribe of dirty words that would make a sailor blush. Indeed, serving in the military only enhanced my repulsive repertoire.

So the other day I decided to see just how many dirty words I could string together without taking a breath. The number was 28.

Nothing to be proud of, mind you. But it's the truth.

Master's degree

As I've grown and matured, of course, I've learned to harness the use of cusswords and use them with discretion.

They can, you see, be very useful when trying to get certain points across to certain people. Especially people who aren't listening or need special motivation.

I'm also in the news business, which means I live in a world where deadlines, gruesome stories and other frustrations bring forth some words you would never see printed in a family newspaper.

And then there's the sports world, where I worked for

many years. This enabled me to earn the equivalent of a master's degree in cursing.

There's a reason TV networks are wary of putting microphones too close to athletes in the heat of competition.

An art form

Naturally, having been raised a mediocre Methodist, I learned the rules and remember one that spoke specifically to this issue. But, quite frankly, it's not the first Commandment I've broken and might not be the last.

Over time, however, I've developed an on-off switch for cussing. I can turn it on when a good curse word will expedite the situation, and turn it off when I'm in polite company.

Some people, however, have no filter and shouldn't be allowed in public with that mouth. Others have favorite little expressions they save for special occasions, usually for shock value.

Little old ladies are among the best. They can look so innocent, then cut you to shreds with a few well-delivered cusswords.

It's an art form, really. One you probably know how to use, too.

Just for a moment, start mentally listing all the dirty words you know. You don't have to say them out loud; just admit that you know them.

And remember, it doesn't mean you're a bad person; it just means you play golf.

I Hear the Train A'coming

Saturday, June 12, 2010

We killed the engine, letting the darkness settle softly around us, as nocturnal noises echoed through the silent swamps of our boyhood.

Regardless of age, there remains a sense of danger deep in the woods at night. At 16, you hear things that haunt your dreams. At 60, you just hope the Jeep starts the next time you turn the key.

If it doesn't, the boy inside you thinks of all the daring things that make life worth living. But the man you grew up to be sees pig paths that wind through cypress swamps where rescue workers find people one day too late.

Still, we parked beneath the stars, next to an old railroad line that sliced through the Savannah River swamp, talking of old times, appreciating friendships that come full circle, laughing aloud, allowing the silence to speak for itself.

Then we heard the whistle.

God's flashlight

Off to the west, beyond the peak of the tallest pines, something lit up the sky, like God's flashlight looking for lost boys.

We knew what was coming — a night train, pulling its long load, bearing down on us, hitting its stride as it swept out of the rolling Georgia hills into the flatlands of South Carolina that lead to the ports and places far beyond.

As it rounded the corner and turned in our direction, the train's powerful lights illuminated the tracks, like two ribbons of fire, gleaming for a mile or more, headed our way, filling our senses with sound and fury seldom experienced in our daily lives.

Anticipating its arrival, we stood on our seats, mere meters from the track, closer than caution dictates, awaiting the mechanical monster that grew in size and sensation as it came roaring toward us.

Night train

As the engine flew past, it sucked oxygen out of the thick night air and we gasped at the speed and sheer excitement of being so close to life and death at the same time.

For a few mesmerizing moments we could not contain our childlike instincts to yell and scream in order to be heard above the rattle and rumble of a hundred rail cars that disappeared as quickly as they came.

We all agreed it was an unexpected exhilaration.

But apparently, it's a guy thing. When we tried to explain this midnight moment to our suspicious spouses, they gave us that look. You know the one — parental, patronizing and perhaps a little perturbed that we put ourselves in such a precarious predicament.

But we just laugh, wink and nod. You had to be there.

Take Me Back to the River

Tuesday, October 6, 2009

Four bends down river from the aptly named Little Hell boat landing, you can hear the sounds of bluegrass music coming from a campsite carved into a high bluff.

Caught in the shimmer of a Carolina moon, the riverbank is lined with fishing boats, pulled snug against the sandy shore, bobbing gently to the rhythms of man and nature.

Armed with guitars, banjos, mandolins and harmonicas, a gaggle of full-grown men from around the Palmetto State gather like swallows on the Savannah River this time of year to celebrate the joy of being alive.

Deep in the glade you can see their tents, blue and orange, sprouting like mushrooms after an autumn rain. But all paths lead to the campfire and cookhouse where fried fish and Frogmore stew are cooked and consumed in a mingling of common interests.

Key among them are the catching of pan-size redbreasts, the drinking of cold beer, the playing of country music and tall tales told and retold upon request.

The soggy bottom

They call themselves the Down The River Gang, a group of 40 that range in age from college boys to graybeards and in respectability from nuclear engineers to guys who exist in that netherworld between opportunities.

To say they span the cultural demographics of our beloved state could be too eloquent for those who participated in the bug-eating contest Friday night.

But it happened. I saw it with my own eyes and wasn't the least bit surprised.

Because this is the soggy bottom where I grew up, along the reaches of a river most know only as the line that separates us from Georgia.

But that curvy wet border is home to those who know the value of spending a weekend in the swamp, camping and laughing with boys you grew up with, men you work with and sons who will carry on when you're gone.

Ongoing ritual

Follow the smell of wood smoke and you'll hear Merle Haggard, Jimmy Buffet, Hank Williams or Jethro Tull, depending on the time of night.

The later, the louder is one way to measure the music. But don't underestimate country boys.

These pipe-fitters and log-splitters can croon a ballad that'll make an undertaker cry, then whisk you away on the Orange Blossom Special.

Saturday's fishing contest fills the fry pans and God made a certain number of men who just love to cook, for which we are grateful.

Surely there are gatherings like this in places I don't know about. But I submit this ongoing ritual as evidence that the real South Carolina has not been completely lost in the real estate rush, as proof that people who live along our two-lane roads remain mostly unaffected by changes along the interstates.

So pull up a log next to the campfire, alongside a friend. The full moon is rising, the air is filled with music and those crickets you hear chirping will be bait come morning.

LIFE'S LESSONS

That Day Changed Everything

Tuesday, August 17, 2010

Thirty years ago this week I pulled into a parking lot, shut off the car engine, put my head on the steering wheel and cried.

On paper, my life looked pretty good. I had a job, I was married, three kids, owned a home, perfectly normal. Except for one thing: I had a merciless drinking problem.

The reality of my life was the story of a small-town boy raised by God-fearing, non-drinking parents. I just didn't know about the broken branches on our family tree where drunks had plunged to unpleasant endings.

Drinking began early in my life. Much too early. We all wanted to grow up fast.

By high school we were seasoned on the sauce. It was part of our culture. Crown Royal and Canadian Club. Southern Comfort and Jack Daniel's.

Beer was abundant, but liquor was quicker.

We thought we were cool. There was no such thing as a DUI in those days.

Various disguises

In college I opened the faucets and let alcohol become the lifeblood of my existence.

My intake was limited only by the availability of money and what I could shamelessly mooch off everybody else.

But I thought everybody drank that way, in excess, to extremes. So I slipped comfortably into the newspaper business, a safe harbor in the old days for poets en route to oblivion.

I never intended to be a drunk. It just came naturally. But we're not all the same. We come in various disguises.

Some are binge drinkers, who suddenly disappear for weeks at a time. Others are functioning alcoholics, who carefully walk the line between discovery and disaster. Then there are the closet drunks, the ones you never suspect because you never see them sober.

I was the kind without an off button. One was too many; a million wouldn't be enough. Once I started, I would drink until they quit making it, or I couldn't stand up, whichever came first.

Had enough

That afternoon in the parking lot, I finally got out of the car and walked into my first Alcoholics Anonymous meeting.

When I walked through that door that day I saw people like me, talking about what life was like then, and what it's like now.

I knew what they meant. Life as a drunk is a complicated, deceitful, disgusting, depreciating way of life. I'd had enough.

I walked up to the first person I came to, stuck out my hand and said, "Hello, my name is Ken. I'm an alcoholic."

That's why I'm alive today.

Recalling the Clunker I Used to Drive

Saturday, January 10, 2009

I came to Charleston in 1984 in a $500 car I paid too much for.

It had been somebody's fishing car, an old, beat-up Volkswagen Squareback.

Be grateful if you don't remember the model.

It was specifically designed for middle-age divorced men to use when they left town.

It represented just the right amount of shame and consumed more oil than gas.

It also lacked a reverse gear, which meant there was no turning back.

I drove that car for two of the most desperate years of my life. One step ahead of family court and two steps behind on the rent.

Sometimes at night, when it was really quiet, I could actually hear it corroding in the salty summer air.

Come morning the front fender would ride to work with me in the back seat, along with my dignity and pride.

Both of us smoked at the time, but it died first, an undignified death on the side of the road, engulfed in flames.

I stood there watching it burn, unable or unwilling to save it.

Raise your hand if you've been there.

Automotive triage

Today I am doing better, but I still slow down when I pass people pulled off on the slender shoulders of life, staring at a car that won't go.

Sometimes the symptoms are visible. Steam rising from the radiator. Smoke billowing from the tailpipe.

Other times, it's something more serious, deep down in the smelly, oily parts of the engine you don't understand.

Mechanics like to whistle through their teeth, wipe a dirty rag across their chin and shake their heads just before delivering the bad news. Overhaul. Rings. Brake job. Unknown electrical issues.

These things, of course, don't come without warning.

You heard the innards grinding when you pulled up steep hills. You tried to ignore the squealing when you ground to a stop.

Sometimes, when you released the clutch, the engine would just conk out and leave you sitting at a green light, your cursing drowned out by a chorus of honking horns.

You live in a world of automotive triage. Fix the fan belt and forgo the left headlight.

Who needs a heater when you have to replace the water hose?

Eventually you're reduced to basics. It cranks. It runs. It's almost legal.

Used tires

Truthfully, you haven't lived the lower end of life until you've bought used tires, wrapped duct tape around a carburetor or tied up the muffler with Christmas tree lights.

If you're poor and without wheels, you know the agony of the used car carousel.

The only thing worse than your present pile of junk is the next bucket of bolts you have to buy. And, without fail, the things that worked on your last car do not work on the next one.

If only you could put three jalopies together to make one almost decent car, you'd have a chance. But you don't.

It's dark and raining and traffic is whizzing past you as you look under the hood, jumper cables in hand, wondering who will come to your rescue.

Maybe somebody like me, who had a car like that once.

HURRICANE HUGO

On the night of September 21, 1989, Hurricane Hugo struck the South Carolina Lowcountry. During that night winds reached 135 miles per hour and a storm surge of 15 feet swept over nearby McClellanville. The eye of Hugo passed over Charleston at midnight.

This devastating hurricane caused more than six billion dollars damage in South Carolina and left thousands homeless.

The greatest cost was the twenty-six lives lost to the storm and its aftermath.

This plaque is dedicated to their memory.

Trudy Whitener Ball, 71
Mt. Pleasant, SC

Terry Capers, 30
Eastover, SC

Amanda Renee Carroll, 8
Conway, SC

Sheryl Christiansen, 41
Averill Park, NY

Leroy Crosby, Jr., 58
Kingstree, SC

Lamont Davis, 1
Mayesville, SC

Florence Bette Dillinger, 65
Georgetown, SC

Harold C. Hutson, 58
Charleston, SC

Brian Arthur Jackson, 38
Fort Lauderdale, FL

Kathleen Ann Kelly Jackson, 41
Fort Lauderdale, FL

Calvin Jackson, Jr. 43
Hartsville, SC

Isiah Mack, 67
Charleston, SC

Arthur McCloud, 54
Charleston, SC

Ras McLellan, Jr., 76
Hamer, SC

Samuel Middleton, 69
Eutawville, SC

Christopher Shea Mounts, 8
Summerville, SC

Robert Lee Page, 59
Charleston, SC

Ernest B. Reeves, 56
Ladson, SC

Manning C. Rodgers, 74
Cassatt, SC

Dyrell Leondra Sinkler, 1
Pinewood, SC

Kelly Denise Sinkler, 3
Pinewood, SC

Teresa Sinkler, 21
Pinewood, SC

Paul Christopher Spencer, 30
James Island, SC

Frierson Wilson, Jr. 32
Dalzell, SC

Samuel Lee Winecoff, Jr., 58
Fort Mill, SC

Norman Dudley Wrenn, 84
Bonneau, SC

Dedicated on the 21st day of September, 1990
Presented to the City of Charleston By WCIV-TV4

Hugo Left a Waterline on Our Lives

Tuesday, September 22, 2009

There is a waterline that runs through my life story, a dark indelible stain that marks a time before and after Hurricane Hugo.

It's like a tattoo, worn out of sight, an initiation into a brotherhood of survivors.

Either you were here, or you weren't.

If you were, you remember the anxious hours as the huge, angry storm grew large on the horizon, slowly engulfing the coastline.

You can still hear the fear in the voices of our leaders as they begged us to leave. You can recall the paralyzing grip of indecision, the doubt, the worry and the inconvenience of it all.

Even those who packed everything from the family photos to their favorite pet into station wagons and minivans remember the dread that came on the night wind.

Vicious visitor

Two decades after darkness drew down on Charleston that September evening, I still have an instinctive, knee-jerk reaction when a storm gathers offshore.

After Hugo, I gained a new and unnerving respect for wind and the devastation it can render when it combines with its favorite playmate, water.

Together, when stirred properly and brought to a boil over a warm southern ocean, they form a brew so awesome in scope the devil himself steps aside to let it pass.

But we had no such option. As a coastal city, sitting steadfast in its path, our only choice was to dance with this vicious visitor.

So we lashed down our loose ends, huddled in dark, protected corners, and waited for the worst.

Around midnight, it arrived.

Sinister silence

Several memories remain vivid in the wake of the storm.

No, not the Ben Sawyer Bridge standing on end, or the boats piled up like toys on Goat Island, or those eerie, empty, concrete slabs where beach houses stood.

Those images are captured forever in famous photos. The things stashed away in my mind are more sensory.

Like those steady, systematic explosions as transformers blew up, flashing green across the cityscape; the squeaking, wrenching rip of tin roofs torn and flapping in the morning breeze; the barking of a dog caught in the collapse of a shaky shed; the sinister silence that fell across the barrier islands; the weary whine of chain saws gnawing their way through fallen debris; the hum of generators in the night; and the sickening sigh of survivors seeing what was left of their homes.

Those are stacked tight with the scent of wet wood; the ubiquitous smell of pine; the taste of sour milk; the wetness of water; the stink of sweat; and the distant fragrance of a hot meal.

Given the choice of living through Hugo or never knowing its power, I would choose the former. Not because there's much joy in the aftermath of such a furious storm. Indeed, joy was more scarce than ice.

What we gained in gracious plenty, however, was a new perspective.

Because of Hugo, there are things I will never take for granted. Likewise, there are things I will never fear.

You Can Leave the Military, But It Never Really Leaves You

Thursday, March 4, 2010

Occasionally, I venture back out to the air base where I'm greeted by an imposing security guard who looks carefully at my identification card, hands it back and says, "Have a good day, tech sergeant."

Every time I go back onto Charleston Air Force Base it feels good to be called by my previous rank, but odd to be in civilian clothes, walking among the servicemen and servicewomen going about their duties as I once did, years ago.

The military, for all its flaws, is a comfort zone for anyone who has ever worn the uniform.

It's a place where you know the rules and know they are enforced. A place where everybody is busy but not too busy to take care of business.

Because there exists behind the gates of every military facility an institutional understanding of respect, order, uniformity, accountability and dedication that becomes part of your marrow and never, ever leaves you.

Reading uniforms

Personally, I miss the fact that you always knew where you stood in the military, and who you were dealing with. That's because you could read somebody's uniform from 20 feet away and know the score.

Service personnel wear their careers on their sleeves, so to speak. When you approach each other, you can read their name tag, examine their rank and, if they are in dress uniform, read their ribbons and know where they've served.

I miss all those little things you take for granted when you're in the ranks, like breaking starch on a set of fatigues fresh from the laundry and standing in a perfectly straight line that looks like a mirror as it stretches to the endless horizon.

I miss the sight of troops marching in the early morn-

ing mist, the sound of boot heels thumping in unison on the sidewalks, the bark of sergeants and the sing-song answers from the squads as they pass by in review.

Hurry Up and Wait

To romanticize military service is to be far removed from its reality, because it's very serious business, especially in times of war.

But I miss the salutes I'd throw at officers and the crisp returns as we crisscrossed on the flight line.

I miss the smell of jet fuel hanging heavily on the night air and the sound of engines roaring down runways and disappearing into the clouds.

I even miss the hurry-up-and-wait mentality that enlisted men gripe about constantly, a masterful invention that bonded people more than they'll ever know or admit.

I miss people taking off their hats when they enter a building, speaking directly and clearly to others and never showing disrespect for rank, race, religion or gender.

Mostly I miss being a small cog in a machine so complex it constantly circumnavigates the Earth and so simple it feeds everyone on time, three times a day, on the ground, in the air or at sea.

Mostly, I don't know anyone who has served who regrets it, and doesn't feel a sense of pride when they pass through those gates and re-enter the world they left behind with their youth.

The Art of Returning Phone Calls

Thursday, February 10, 2011

I remember the day I learned the lesson about returning phone calls.

I was young, not long out of college, working at another newspaper and feeling pretty good about myself until my managing editor called me into his office.

In his hand was one of those pink message slips from days gone by. Yes, Virginia, there was a time before voice mail when people actually took messages and wrote them down.

So there was Charlie Byars, the kind of guy whose list you don't want to be on, waving this piece of paper and saying, "This guy says he's left you three messages and you haven't returned his call. Why not?"

I immediately said I was so busy and had so much to do and....

"Well, you'll have plenty of time on your hands if you don't return this call," he bellowed. "It's not only your job, it's the right thing to do."

Passionate audience

More than 35 years later, I still heed his advice when the nice lady on my voice mail says, "You have 16 new messages."

Some, of course, are just routine. Some are complimentary. Others are not.

But I always call them back. Always.

It was really fun back when I was a sports columnist. When you write sports you attract a very passionate audience that's not shy about telling you what they think of what you wrote the day before.

The best ones usually came in about 2:30 in the morning when somebody was inebriated and decided to let me have it in rather profane and vulgar terms.

Most didn't leave a name or number, of course, but Caller-ID gave me all I needed to know.

Haggard, hung-over

When I'd call the number back the next morning, a raspy voice would answer, and I'd say, "Good morning, this is Ken Burger at *The Post and Courier* newspaper, and I'd like to thank you for the message you left for me last night."

After an awkward silence, a haggard, hung-over soul would say, "Oh man, is this really Ken Burger?"

"Yes," I'd say. "And I really appreciate you taking the time to call and tell me what you thought about that column."

Another pause would follow, and I'd hear, "Hey, man, like you know, that wasn't me saying all that stuff."

"Really?"

"Yeah man, you know, that must've been my brother-in-law. He gets drunk and comes over here and uses my phone. It must have been him."

"Well," I'd say, "please tell your brother-in-law I appreciate it, even though some of those things he suggested I do are physically impossible."

Eventually, the guy would laugh, 'fess up, and we'd become friends before it was all over.

Calling people back, you see, is a sign of respect, even if they don't deserve it.

'Be Sweet': Good Advice for Anyone

Sunday, June 19, 2011

I wonder if obnoxious people think the rest of us are suckers.

Do they think our pleasant dispositions, our generosity, our sincere caring, our willingness to help, our genuine interest in our fellow human beings is somehow an invitation for abuse?

When they take advantage of others, push to the head of the line, ignore the rules and cheat the system, do they believe they're doing the right thing?

Do they think being loud and bullying people is the best way to live their lives? Do they believe the rest of us are here for their amusement?

Is that the way they were raised?

Minding manners

Every time I left the house, my mother used to holler out the back door for me to "be sweet," no matter where I was going.

Those two simple words summarized my parents' expectations for my behavior.

I was supposed to conduct myself at all times in a manner that not only reflected well on them, but myself, and everybody in my family. I was expected to be nice to everybody, regardless of color, age, or position in the world.

I knew to address people in a pleasant tone, to open doors for ladies, to respect my elders, to watch out for younger children, to be on time, to be presentable, to look both ways before crossing the street, and to speak in complete sentences.

Yes sir and yes ma'am were integral parts of my vocabulary. I didn't talk back. I spoke when spoken to. I played fair. I didn't say bad words in public. I stayed awake in church. I minded my manners at the table. And I never,

ever thought of arguing with my daddy.

Two little words

Maybe if I'd been raised somewhere else by different parents I'd be a totally different person.

Maybe I'd be tougher, meaner, more conniving, less trustworthy, more self-centered, sneakier, more suspicious, and somehow better prepared to deal with the harsh realities of life.

Maybe I wouldn't care what other people thought of me, or if they got a fair deal, or even if they lived or died.

Maybe I'd think only of myself, disregarding others' needs, trash somebody's reputation in order to improve my own, lie when it suited my needs, or ignore other people's feelings because they don't really matter.

Or perhaps I'd drive like I was the only one on the highway, believing my destination was more important than all those other people doing the speed limit and driving defensively, because of people like me.

Maybe I'd interrupt people when they were talking, not pay attention to someone when they tried to explain something, or belittle someone because they were physically or mentally different.

Personally, I feel sorry for people like that. I guess their mothers never told them to "be sweet," two little words that can make all the difference in life.

Don't Be Afraid to Fail in Life

Saturday, May 28, 2011

ESTILL — The graduation season is upon us, a time to celebrate success and bask in all the optimism that goes with it.

In caps and gowns and smiles and tassels, this year's graduates embark on a journey that leads down a path of no return, to places unexplored and circumstances unexpected.

And, chances are, they won't all turn out well.

Friday night, I stood here before the Class of 2011 at Patrick Henry Academy, a fresh-faced bunch who had been told of how successful this boy from nearby Allendale had become. Big-city columnist, award-winning author, blah, blah, blah.

I'm sure they expected the usual speech about setting goals and reaching for the stars. But what they got was quite different. It was the rest of the story. Because, when it comes to failure, I'm an expert.

Unvarnished truth

While life looks easy in retrospect, it's more complex when you're actually living it. In fact, it's downright difficult and often takes turns you never anticipated.

So I told these students the unvarnished truth about myself, in hopes they would understand that it's OK to flop. For me, failure has been a companion I've learned to live with.

Like a lot of kids, I suffered the common failures of youth like not being very good at sports. But that was just the beginning.

When I was their age, I was kicked off my high school newspaper for rebelling against authority. I also got kicked off my college newspaper for the same reason, which foretold an interesting pattern.

As a student, I was a complete mess. My teachers said I didn't apply myself. I said I didn't test well. Mainly because I didn't know the answers.

That became painfully obvious when I didn't have four numbers in my SAT score, which meant I had a hard time getting into college and an even harder time getting out. In fact, I flunked out. Eventually, I graduated, but I was dead last in my class. Hey, somebody has to be, right?

Along the way, I picked up a nasty little drinking problem. While alcoholism is not a personal failure, it certainly looks that way when you're living it. Thankfully, I quit drinking at age 30, but not without leaving damage in my wake.

That would be enough for most people, but I wasn't done.

Puzzle pieces

I've always had a love-hate relationship with the newspaper business, leaving it twice for all the wrong reasons. Once I bombed as a salesman. Another time I went broke in public relations.

Then there were the divorces, four of them, of which I was the only common denominator. As a result, I was never nominated for father of the year. Fortunately, my three well-adjusted children gave me a mulligan, for which I'm forever grateful.

Today my resume doesn't list those failures. But they are important pieces of the puzzle that is me.

So remember, it's not that you fail, or even how often you fail, but how you handle failure that ultimately determines your success.

When It's Your Turn to Paddle

Tuesday, May 17, 2011

The world is made up of two kinds of people — givers and takers. As a regular reader and championship-caliber person, you are probably the former rather than the latter.

Chances are you give back to the community through some type of volunteer effort. Some do it through their church. Others contribute through various service organizations. Some just have a knack for finding something that needs doing and doing it, without regard to recognition or reward.

Obviously, there is no end to the need.

Even before the recent recession, there were severe pockets of poverty and neglect that needed attention. There were people who, through no fault of their own, or maybe even through fault of their own, were in need of a helping hand.

In recent years, those needs have escalated as unemployment has soared and state and federal funds dried up overnight.

It's in times like this, however, when we are at our best. And you don't have to look far to find examples.

Ordinary people

Right here in the Lowcountry, there are hundreds of groups dedicated to keeping people from slipping through the cracks.

This is when ordinary people do extraordinary things, like feeding the hungry, housing the homeless, caring for the sick, protecting the children, and looking out for the elderly, just to mention a few.

There are numerous groups dedicated to filling these needs. To list them would require this entire page, and we still would leave somebody out. Suffice it to say, we are good at collective charity.

But there are a million other good deeds that occur

daily, even hourly, in our communities that often go unnoticed.

Same boat

In almost every neighborhood there's someone who looks after the old lady who is homebound and can't get to the grocery store. Or the guy who cuts the grass for a handicapped couple who can no longer afford to have it done.

You probably know someone who makes a point of cooking a little extra for a family who runs out of money before they run out of month.

Or the lady who gives her aging neighbor rides to the doctor, occasionally cleans the house, or simply holds a hand when it needs holding.

And show me a business in the Lowcountry that doesn't contribute financially to good causes, sponsor youth athletic teams, and come to the aid of the community in times of need.

And it's not just here.

All across America, in the wake of terrible tornadoes, volunteers appear in small, devastated towns with chain saws and aid without being asked.

Along the rain-swollen Mississippi River, where flood waters are rising, people pitch in to help friends and total strangers, because it's the right thing to do.

Bottom line, when it comes to getting through this thing called life, we're all in the same boat. And sometimes, it's just your turn to paddle.

SOUTHERN SENSATIONS

Sounds of Southern Summer

Tuesday, July 21, 2009

Back when inside felt like outside, screen doors were our best defense against insects and other varmints that insisted on living within rather than without.

Created in the 1880s, this magical metal mesh was the only thing between us and the relentless summer heat.

Back before air conditioning threw up the invisible wall that separates us from everything and each other, screen doors served as protection. They kept bad things out but still let good things in.

Things like a gentle breeze off the water, the sound of crickets at night, a bullfrog bellowing in the lily pads, a dog barking way down a dirt road, a car passing by late at night or a young girl giggling in the dark.

These are just a few of the things I miss since we buttoned up and battened down the hatches of our homes.

If you'd just crack a door or open a window, you'd be surprised to learn what you're missing.

Gnat's wings

There is no sound as Southern as a screen door slamming behind a little boy on his way out into the world of wonder.

Such doors in my childhood were made of wood with wire screen stapled down the top and sides to keep it in place.

The mesh itself was smaller than a gnat's wings and strung tight. But over time, the elements and occupants took a toll. Sometimes the screen sagged, tore loose at the corners and flapped in the breeze.

Even in the best of homes there might be holes in the screen, created by young cowpokes in a hurry, an umbrella carried askew or somebody's errant elbow.

But mostly they were worn down by use, flung open by hands coming and going, then pulled slowly shut by a rusty spring that allowed it to swing only so far before it slapped back into place.

Which is why they didn't always fit well, and often squeaked and creaked every time they were used.

No pretension

A best kind of screen door, of course, was not perfectly painted. It had well-worn spots near the handle and elsewhere on its wooden face.

Because of constant use, the door was sometimes wobbly and didn't always fit tight in the corners, unless you used the little latch to secure it.

Screen doors on old houses simply had character and told a story about those who lived there.

There's no pretension in a screen door. It just has a welcoming way about it. Like the smell of fresh-baked pies pouring out, or the sound of good friends walking up the sidewalk to visit.

Just the sound of them swinging open and shut brings back memories of a time when we knew when our neighbors pulled into their driveway, when the milkman came by in the early morning, how often the town sprayed for mosquitoes, if the ice cream truck was coming, when it was raining, and if the kids were still playing in the sprinkler in the back yard.

I really miss that.

Don't you?

Recalling the Porches of Our Past

Tuesday, April 26, 2011

Somewhere in our haste to subdivide society, we eliminated porches and replaced them with nothing that comes close to filling the need to sit a spell and watch the world go by.

That's what front porches were used for in a time when people passed by slow enough to speak to, when you knew your next-door neighbor, the family down the street, and the lady who pushed her baby in a stroller every morning, just before nap time.

Mostly the porches were screened, which cast an eerie reflection when the sun slanted a certain way and a breeze made the mesh roll ever-so slightly like waves from a distant boat.

Upon these porches the chairs were wicker and there might be a rope hammock in the corner, or a slatted swing that hung from screws sunk deep into ceiling studs.

It's where people came to catch an afternoon breeze, shell beans, rock babies, gossip, play guitar, and pass time before the sun went down, or better yet, in the cool of a soft summer night.

Paving the past

Front porches were prevalent in the Palmetto State before we scraped away the trees and planted endless rows of look-alike houses with optional floor plans, carports and red-stained decks.

In the Piedmont, you could sit in a rocker and survey the sloping scenery, feel the cool air spilling down the mountainside, tell ghost stories, and pull a sweater over your shoulders before the moon rose above the hilltops.

In the Midlands, porches were festooned with flowers, a place where bees buzzed, and the infernal heat was stirred slowly by paddles of a ceiling fan.

In the Lowcountry, the screens served as mosquito netting, stretched tight to keep the menacing marauders at bay, but transparent enough to let children see the lightning bugs play on a thick, luscious lawn.

Even our beach houses, the ones with wrap-around porches, are becoming a memory dimmed by time, somewhat forgotten in the rush to air-condition the planet and pave what was left of our past.

Simple Splendor

We can blame developers, architects, commutes, and driveways for the disappearance of porches.

We can even point fingers at our auto-driven lifestyle, our garage-door mentality, or our general lack of laziness.

But screened porches, in all their simple splendor, are still out there, sagging, torn and tattered, behind moss-draped trees, down winding dirt roads, along riverbanks, in places left behind.

If only we had known what we were losing when we tore them away and let them succumb to the changing times, we might have let them live on, in modern design, a salute to the way we were, a quiet place to read a book or take a nap.

While some new houses have porches and pretend to placate our past, it's just not the same when you're looking at your neighbor's swing set.

There's No Place Like the Fair

Tuesday, November 3, 2009

A little girl is riding on her daddy's shoulders, eyes ablaze as they approach the flashing neon world that is the Coastal Carolina Fair.

So much to see. So little time.

First you must inhale the essence of the fair, those fertile aromas that rise from the horses in the rodeo pen, the elephant and camels, the donkeys in the petting zoo.

It all mixes so well with those from the cows and goats in the agricultural building.

From the moment you walk in, your senses are under assault. There are bright lights from the Ferris wheel and all those spinning rides that leave you weak-kneed and wobbly when you try to walk away.

They're all just a blur in the background, distractions that come from every direction at once. A helicopter swooping overhead, loud music blaring from every attraction, and the ubiquitous screams of children stimulated by sugar and excitement.

Culinary concoctions

And there's food, lots of food. Walking down the midway, you're immersed in the best and worst culinary concoctions known to man.

Cotton candy, cheese fries, chili fries, fried bologna, deep-fried MoonPies, BBQ, sausages, hot dogs, elephant ears, fried turkey legs, deep-fried peanut butter and jelly sandwiches, funnel cakes, candy apples, roasted corn, egg rolls, calzones, pizzas, blooming onions, cheese sticks, peanuts, corn dogs and candy by the pound.

Once you've consumed all that, you're ready to ride the rides, play the games and witness things you can find only at the fair.

Like the world's smallest horse or the 300-pound snake. Then there are games of skill, games of luck, dancing girls and the house of mirrors. How about a psychic reading for only $3?

Or you could listen to Percy Sledge sing "When A Man Loves A Woman" as you dance in the aisle with your sweetheart.

Best first date

Because fairs aren't just for kids. Going to the fair is probably the best first date a couple could ever have.

There's nothing like taking those silly pictures you'll keep for a lifetime, or trying to toss a basketball through a tiny rim, or a ball through the eyes in a smiley face, or acting silly on the bumper cars.

But the best thing about the fair is that people are smiling.

Where else can you pet a Brahman bull, purchase cheap jewelry, get hypnotized, buy T-shirts and talk to beekeepers and taxidermists in the same place? There's even a group called the Charleston Rabbit Breeders Association. How hard can that job be?

In between exhibits, you can play the game of trying to distinguish the pickpockets from the undercover cops. Funny how they have a knack for finding each other in a crowd.

Which is a skill you wish you had when you're walking around the parking lot, lost, trying to remember where you parked your car, with a sleepy little girl on your shoulders.

So Many Reasons to Love Golf

Sunday, April 27, 2008

I love golf.

Absolutely love it.

I love the way my clubs rattle when I take them out of the trunk, the way my golf shoes feel, the softness of the glove, the sound of Velcro peeling and tightening at the wrist, the sag of an old Seagram's sack that holds my watch and cell phone.

I love the mood in the clubhouse, the pastel shirts folded neatly on a table, the multi-colored hats aligned on the shelf, the idle banter between golfers, every individual sleeve of balls, every bag of tees.

I love the way a golf cart beeps when you back up, jerks when you start forward, goes a little faster than you expected and clicks when you lock the brake.

I love the idea of the practice range, the ball dispensing machines, the little plastic baskets, the guy in the picker-upper-mobile, the perception of progress, the first wedge and the last drive you hit.

I love the putting green, like a dance floor, where you drop three balls, steer clear of each other's space, make some, miss some, scoop them up and walk away like you've learned something.

Fairways, frog hair

I love the first tee, the way starters greet and give you instructions, the concept of cart-path-only, the beauty of the 90-degree rule, the feel of a brand new scorecard and those little pencils without erasers.

I love the smell of freshly mowed fairways in the morning, the bending at the waist, the one-legged ballet, balancing your weight on your driver, sticking a tall white tee into the ground, placing a ball on top and believing this is going to be the day.

I love the sound of a practice swing, the moment of

address, the waggle and the first inch of the back swing from which there is no return.

I love the exact moment of impact, the bend in the shaft, the imperceptible grunt of human effort, the follow through and the inevitable pose.

I love watching the ball leave at high speed, climb, reach its zenith, diminish in the distance, fall, roll and lie quietly on the ground.

I love the bad shots, too, the splash of white sand, the kaplunk of blue water, the hollow konk of old oak, the hide-and-seek games in high rough.

I love the way foursomes hit, in order of distance from the green without being told, the selection of irons, the judging of wind, the good intentions of each earnest swing.

I love gap wedges, new grips, head covers, sprinkler heads, playing with strangers, the handicap system, ball washers, hazard stakes, drop areas and the white tees.

I love filling divots, fixing ball marks, avoiding your partner's putting line, and greenskeepers who stop mowing while you hit.

I love greenside bunkers with high lips, frog hair, fast greens, the clank of a pin being dropped, sand wedges left on the putting surface, putts that break left, putts that break right, downhill putts, uphill putts, and those devilish putts that don't break at all.

Caddies, chili dogs

I love all manner of ball marks, like pocket change and plastic things that snap on your glove, hang on your pocket or clip on your cap.

I love putters that come in all shapes and sizes, like people, only stranger and less willing to accept blame, until banished to the way-back part of your car trunk.

I love the purr of a putt rolling against the grain, the way the logo wobbles when the ball slows down, the anxiety it creates when it gets close, and the oh-so-sweet sound when it finds the bottom of the cup.

I love one-putts, two-putts, three-putts, backhanded jabs, good-goods, gimmes and the ones just outside the leather.

I love the fist-pumps, the head-nods, the eye-rolls and the sighs of relief that follow any made putt.

I love the three-finger pickup from the hole, the player who always puts the flag back in the hole and the ones who never do.

I love writing numbers on the scorecard, adding up scores at the turn, a good golf-course chili dog and the eternal promise of the back nine.

I love the honesty of golf, the cruelty of stroke and distance penalties, searching for an opponent's lost ball, walking with a caddie, the humility of triple bogeys, playing it where it lies and counting every shot.

I love the presence of laughter, the absence of anger, the camaraderie, the pranks, the golf jokes, and the beer cart girls.

I love the 18th hole, the handshakes all around, the excuses, the could-have-beens, the should-have-beens, and how we're all going to do better next time.

Because we love golf.

Absolutely love it.

Sand, Sun, Surf, and Serenity

Saturday, August 1, 2009

There is something universally soothing about a long walk on the beach. The crashing of waves, the wind in your hair.

No matter how far you come to be here, the sensation is the same. Sea gulls gliding overhead. Brown pelicans plunging into the water. Shrimp boats on the distant horizon.

Little wonder we lose ourselves in the daydream, strolling the ocean's edge, splashing saltwater as we go, feeling the tug of an unseen undertow.

South Carolina has its faults, but our natural beauty makes up for some of our flaws.

We are blessed with long stretches of sand, smooth underfoot, reaching for miles along the sloping shoulders of our state.

It's no wonder so many flock to the Palmetto State this time of year. The beaches are packed with people in various forms of relaxation, soaking up the summer sun, reading, napping, allowing the rhythm of the tides to take control of their soul.

From Surfside to Seabrook, Pawleys to the Isle of Palms, Myrtle Beach to Murrells Inlet, Kiawah to Crescent Beach, Folly to Litchfield and Garden City to Cherry Grove, we live in a wondrous place.

Scent of sunscreen

The beach at dawn is almost deserted, except for a man and his dog, running in tandem as the light breaks over the eastern rim.

The ocean, always in motion, scarcely notices as it draws back across the canvas it covered the night before.

Gone are love notes scratched in the sand, castles constructed by children and the footprints of a thousand tourists on a moonlight stroll.

Busy are the shorebirds, breakfasting on the edge of a sudsy brew that bubbles with each incoming wave. So too, a pair of osprey that hover above, preparing to dive on an unsuspecting school of shiny silver fish.

The air is still and fresh, untouched by the scent of sunscreen. The beach is clean, except for tiny shells and scattered sweeps of seaweed.

From the south, coming quickly, a helicopter thumps into view, doors open to the rushing wind, as our coastal guardians prepare for another day.

Old Bay brine

By late afternoon, the crush of cars create a parking lot, and the spill of humanity huddles under umbrellas, sprouting like colorful mushrooms along the beach.

Kids, immune to danger, splash in the surf where older men, ever the optimists, cast lines to snag shark and other things that mothers, always vigilant, fear the most.

Between blankets spread at random, little girls play hopscotch and teenaged boys throw footballs against the wind, as older girls, in bikinis, pretend to ignore them completely.

Slowly but surely, the sea reclaims the people's playground, chasing them back to beach houses where wild shrimp boil in Old Bay brine and laughter carries from one front porch to another, like sea birds soaring downwind.

In the distance, the sky is streaked with low-lying clouds, the summer sun sets the sky ablaze, dolphins roll silently by, and the ocean, always in motion, scarcely notices at all.

Capturing the City's Cadence

Saturday, June 19, 2010

Listen carefully as dawn breaks over The Battery. Squawking seabirds combine with the sounds of lapping waves on the rocks below to announce another day in paradise has begun.

Charleston in the early morning hours is a symphony of sounds, from birds chirping high in the palmetto trees to the perpetual padding of joggers along the seawall.

Down a side street, an air conditioner kicks into gear but does not drown out the distant bark of a dog pulling his master along the quiet sidewalk.

High above the Carolina Yacht Club, flags salute the Cooper River side of the harbor while halyards clang against idle masts in the City Marina on the Ashley.

As our city yawns and stretches, the bells of St. Michael's toll, a ringing reminder of every morning that has come and gone and will come again, with or without us.

First wink

Behind high walls, fountains trickle, barely audible above the spitting sprinklers spraying thirsty lawns.

Always silent are the ancient graveyards, where they've heard it all before.

Turn a corner and sparrows fly, squirrels scamper and a cyclist whizzes by, tires whirring on the pavement as he passes.

Men with badges enter the courthouse through a side door, as a machine spits out tickets to the parking garage.

Colonial Lake is a stillshot but for a ripple that barely causes the tympanic membrane to tremble.

In White Point Garden, oyster-shell paths announce your approach, making a hoot owl most unhappy.

Splashing water awaits squealing children in Waterfront Park. Nearby, groggy passengers disembark a cruise ship that drones in its berth like a hummingbird anxious to leave.

Down the street, workers systematically empty parking meters that sound like city slot machines.

Clip-clop

On Meeting Street, garbage trucks idle restlessly and city buses hiss and bow as they take on passengers.

Oak leaves rustle on the sidewalk along that shady stretch near the art museum, and there's the unmistakable clink of coffee cups coming from Toast.

On East Bay, beer trucks line up to refill coolers drained the night before, and vendors unload their wares in the Market for another day in the trinket trade.

Overhead, silhouetted against a bright blue sky, an Air Force C-17 slips down through white puffy clouds, yet the sound of a squeegee on a restaurant window prevails.

In the lobby of Charleston Place, luggage wheels roll across marbled floors while a cappuccino machine in Starbucks whirs across the street.

On Liberty, a shop owner turns the key and opens for business as the summer silence surrounds the Cistern on the campus of the College of Charleston.

Nearby, bacon sizzles on the grill at Jack's Cafe, and by midmorning, the ubiquitous clip-clop of carriage horses completes the quiet cacophony that is an early morning in Charleston.

Sunsets and Other Sensations

Tuesday, June 7, 2011

Across a marshy expanse, just beyond the tree line, where the tidal creek bends and the shrimp boats dock, the last rays of a long summer day lie low on a shimmering horizon.

The red-hot sphere that stoked another sun-splashed South Carolina day seems to be falling fast, as we roll over, trying to hide our face and dream of seashells and such.

That we can look westward and witness this consistent climax creates awe at the simple majesty of a very complicated world.

Thus we sit on docks and decks, patios and porches, with sandy feet and sunburned shoulders, watching young kids pull the crab trap, just one more time, and tune out teenagers who tease each other and test that very last nerve.

Because there is always that one moment when every-one turns, suddenly realizing the urgency, and watches the great orb disappear below the horizon.

A gauzy glow

Sometimes clouds scud low across treetops, scattering shafts of light across the scene where dolphins roll in quiet streams and seabirds sail silently by.

Then there's Mother Nature's geometric trick, the one where she bounces light off the water, creating a shiny sheet across the creek that lights it up like a neon sign.

On hazy days, when the sun rides low and takes on a gauzy glow, you can feel the air cool slightly as the breeze imperceptibly turns with the outgoing tide.

And somewhere deep in the marsh grass, a heron flushes, wings pulling hard against the humid air, fleeing an unseen threat, which, heaven forbid, might be you.

This is the time to stop, switch off the electronic aggravations, and breathe in the end of the day. Be it the best, the worst, or somewhere in between, it's the only one that matters at the moment.

Colors explode

The lower the sun dips, the quieter it gets along the shoreline, a pact no doubt, struck long ago between the world of water and the sun which warms it.

All too soon the light will fade, bending colors like a giant prism, taking its last bow, inch by inch, until it pauses on the rim, slowly sinking, winking, saying goodbye without regret or promise.

The same sun that caused us to squint into windshields, crank the air conditioning up high, and cover our skin with protective goo is about to disappear in the blink of an egret's eye.

It's in those final moments, when the colors explode, backlit against a threatening thunderhead, that we connect with an astronomic truth, the one that tells us it will be back tomorrow, and the day after that, and the day after that, we hope.

Thus we honor its dramatic departure, knowing the darkness is temporary, that the sun will rise again to light our way, and set most graciously at the end of each day for our personal, ephemeral pleasure.

AFTERWORD

There was a time in my life when I thought writing was a parlor trick, something I could do to entertain people, something that didn't take much effort or thought. It began as bad poetry, an adolescent effort to make words sound like bells in a chapel, or hooves on a muddy road, or chatter in church. That's what writing is to me, really. While the words and their meanings are imperative to the translation of the art, it is the sound that makes it art.

I didn't know that, of course, when I was a little kid scribbling verses or penning short stories in grammar school.

All I knew was that I liked the feeling of putting words in order, shaping them to fit the mood I was in or the one I wanted to present. This hobby hobbled alongside my studies in math and science and sociology, which usually got short shrift during my academic years.

Mostly I wanted to write stories, have people read them, then tell me how nice they were. People are nice to children with dreams. And it's a good thing. Because they are like elegant soap bubbles that float precariously above the sharp edges of reality, ready to be popped by a single, unthinking statement, an offhand remark or someone's uncontrollable urge to cause harm. Death of a dream, in fact, is a sad occasion that often goes unnoticed. It's simply cast aside, considered unimportant, and goes dormant if not rescued.

I often describe myself as having lived a charmed life, which I have. Despite the ravages of alcoholism, divorce, bankruptcy, cancer, and loves lost and found and lost again, I have always managed to maintain a steady flow of prose. I don't always know where it comes from. It's just always been there when I reached for it, which was often during a 40-year career in the newspaper business. Over time, I grew to trust it like the next breath. Without question. Without fear that it might one day disappear.

In fact, it's quite the contrary. Since I retired from the business of meeting daily deadlines, I've learned that the writing faucet is hard, if not impossible, to turn off. That it's not just a parlor trick. It's actually like an internal organ that keeps pumping out ideas and thoughts and rhymes and reasons to write things down, even the most mundane things that happen in life, which can be the most revealing.

These days I compose a blog (www.kenburgerblog.com), which gives me a bucket to catch what flows from that leaky faucet. Some days it's funny. Some days it's not. But almost every day it empties the brain of those pesky questions without answers, ideas without homes or observations that deserve to be noticed.

I've also managed to finish two novels, "Swallow Savannah" and "Sister Santee," which much to my surprise, have done well. The next one, "Salkehatchie Soup," will serve my alliteration fetish while picking at another scab on the skin of our beloved Palmetto State.

"Baptized In Sweet Tea," for instance, is like an old pickup truck that allows me to rumble down the dirt roads of my youth and paint a picture of what it was like growing up in South Carolina in the middle of the 20th century, after the good war of our fathers and before the bad war that decimated my generation. Through it all, I've learned a lot about myself. Maybe that's the real wisdom that comes with writing: The fact that it forces open doors that might not otherwise be opened.

To that end, it has been a continuous release of soul-searching solace throughout my life. Now, in my early 60s, I've come to know that little kid who wrote poetry much better. He was a lucky soul, indeed. To live in a place where everyday people do everyday things, and to have the ability to capture them in thought and word and deed. Writing, you see, is not just about words. It's about perspective. It's about having the courage to believe that what you have to say might be worth reading. That perhaps you are the only person in the whole wide world who can say it just the right way, so it matters to somebody, somewhere. In the end, whenever that comes, if someone hears my name and it jogs a memory or causes a pause because of something I wrote in a column or penned amid thousands of pages of prose, perhaps they will turn to a friend and say, "You know, he was a pretty good writer." Which is all I ever wanted to be.

PHOTOGRAPHY

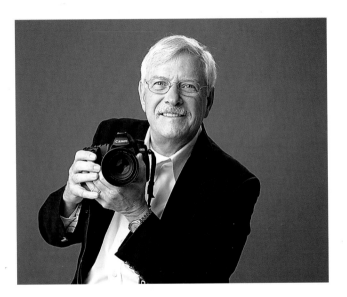

David Gentry is a Psychology Professor at the College of Charleston. He was born in Florence, Alabama and spent his earlier years in Alabama and Tennessee. After he received a bachelor's degree in aerospace engineering at Georgia Tech, he worked for NASA in Houston at the Johnson Spacecraft Center during the Gemini and Apollo programs. He then returned to Georgia Tech to complete a PhD in psychology. He and his wife, Dr. Martha Watson, live on Johns Island, S.C. where they welcome children and grandchildren for regular visits. David's avocation is digital photography with special interest in sports, travel, nature and portraits.

For more on David and his photos, please visit his website http://davidgentry.photoshelter.com.

Additional photos:
Chris Hanclosky, *The Post and Courier* - pages 52, 54